Solar Music

poems by

Elaine Alarcón

Finishing Line Press
Georgetown, Kentucky

Solar Music

ACKNOWLEDGMENTS

"Ghost Bikes, Inc.," "Mexico City Sleight of Hand," and "Once in
Tepotzotlán" appeared in ASKEW;

"The Circular Valley" and "Atala Addresses Her Aztec Gods" appeared in
SALT; "Adoration of Remedios Varo" also appeared in SALT under a
slightly different title;

"Granada" and "Apotheosis at Viznar" appeared in SPILLWAY;

"Lorca Suite" appeared in SOLO VOYAGE:

"Granada," "Grandmother Granada," "Oxnard—Granada—Oxnard, et.
al"; "Trip Advisor: Flamenco Show at *Le Chien Andalou*"; "Apotheosis
at Viznar"

Publisher: Leah Huete de Maines
Editor: Christen Kincaid
Cover Art: Peg Quinn
Author Photo: Barclay Totten
Cover Design: Elizabeth Maines McCleavy

Order online: www.finishinglinepress.com
also available on amazon.com

Author inquiries and mail orders:
Finishing Line Press
PO Box 1626
Georgetown, Kentucky 40324
USA

Contents

Ghost Bikes, Inc. 1

Adoration of Remedios Varo 3

Granada 4

Grandmother Granada 6

Oxnard—Granada—Oxnard *et. al* 8

Trip Advisor: Flamenco Show at Le Chien Andalou 10

Apotheosis at Viznar 12

Mexico City Sleight of Hand 13

Once in Tepotzotlán 15

Atala Adresses Her Aztec Gods 17

The Circular Valley 18

Amilcar Beach, Tunisia 20

Arab Vespers 22

Matisse's "Window at Tangier 1912" 23

North Africa 25

What is the Word for Surrender? 27

Death in Tunisia 28

Ghost Bikes, Inc.

Here is an old map in delicate colors
of holy spots in Oxnard;
these are the stations of the cross.

For a ghost bike, go north on Ventura Road
or south on Rose, just past the high school
and Strawberry Meadows.

Here, slathered in white paint like a papier-mâché
bike, laden with plastic daisies, roses,
and tissue paper marigolds
whose scent will never lead
home the dead's wandering ghosts
on Day of the Dead,
ghost bike leans into a fence
and a NO PARKING sign,
frozen pedals punctuating
an ellipsis.

For death by locomotive
follow Oxnard Boulevard
to the Sunkist factory
abutting the track and imagine
a small white cross
long forgotten for Arturo's brother
taking a shortcut in front of Amtrak,
the photo finish capturing
Arturo's stricken face.

Go north along the same stretch
to the shrine of the palm tree
feted by balloons
and teddy bears bleached
by the sun and studded
with bird droppings;

here a police chase hurtled a Bronco
with its little birthday girl
into the tree a block away.
The tree sustained no injuries.

Other spots on the map grace
crossroads where spirits linger
beside crosses and withered bouquets;
these are old deaths also,
as sanctified by their dusty colors
on memory's fraying map.

At Rice and Channel Island
a girl's nude body was thrown
into a ditch besides the strawberry field
whose pungent marigold borders
stave off insects but not murder.
When it's absent I miss the bouquet
her sister leaves
by the plain little cross
at this intersection where cars stream
by and half-naked cross country
runners take no notice.

It has been a long time
since roses garnished this corner
and longer still since blood dried
and mingled with dirt
the wind has blown over the fields.

For additional wonders, simply follow
the crosses on the map;
you can't miss them.

Adoration of Remedios Varo

Surrealist painter
Catalonia 1908—1963 Mexico City

Varo, goddess, I wish I had known you in Spain
and also your cat, Mimesis, as it looked up
from inside the floorboards for blessing;
and the woman evolving from a chair,
then flowing into Aurora-of-the-Lanes,
hair and gown fluttering with radiance,
her soul full of bird starlight.
Yes, I wish I had known you all.

I wish I had known you in Paris
after you fled Barcelona
and its useless alchemist in his tower
with razor eyes, weaving
the black and white checkered floor
of his monk's cell, homage to Franco.

And later, after you had fled Hitler,
I wish I had known you in Mexico City,
net in hand for catching stars,
with the nightingale moon
already caught and nesting in its little cage.

I would have wandered D.F.'s lapis
streets with you, your votary,
till we found the vagabond flute player
and his flaming feline familiar tucked
inside his unicycle cape. I would have eaten
at your table while a galaxy of plates spun
a helix of candle shadows; I would have sailed
upon your conversation in a boat of white heron.

Varo, I ache for your baptism and the journeys
you took, driving your motorized waistcoat
through the misty wood to Orinoco
searching for solar music.

Granada

In the garden of Manuel de Falla
quinces and pomegranates
sweeten the wind
threading cypresses and the Vega beyond,
smoke from tobacco farms
pluming at the margins.
Music rises from the rooftops
like incense, escaped spirits
of de Falla's harpsichord flowing
outward from his windows, prayer
cascading through nasturtiums
to bless my encounters with his sonatas
decades earlier.

All no less stunning
than the forlorn young woman
on the cathedral plaza,
her voice a night river
calling over the traffic—
poignant, hermetic, insistent—
the little match girl now grown
striking her fire;
blocks away her dark song, still heard
without microphone,
soars and loops
over the traffic
like prophecy, like Jericho.

And music also rises
in the street below my window
on Calle Tablas
at all hours of the night
from students passing back and forth—
sometimes a male chorus,
sometimes a female,
sometimes both together, exuberant.

In this once war-torn city
where Lorca was arrested
in this very house,
music, not blood,
now flows in the street
snaking in and out of consciousness,
as the accordion player
below my window
pleats the air with chuffing sounds,
until, finally,
I hear "*Cielito Lindo*" through the traffic,
a tune my father strummed on his guitar
when I was his little minx
and danced on our front step
for the sky, imagining I was Spain.

Grandmother Granada

From my hotel window
I listen for the accordion player's song,
sacred messenger
entrusted with mystery.
I long to catch his eye.
Once I even tried to follow him
before he vanished into one
of Granada's many little canyons.
Sometimes he plays by the cathedral
punctuating the cold slumber
of Ferdinand and Isabella,
Catholic furies driving Moors
from the Alhambra's purple iris
and oleander wood.

But tonight the accordion serenade
beneath my window
is a tune from my father's guitar
I once danced to in faux Flamenco,
swinging the hem of my green bathrobe,
dancing as my grandmother once danced
in her Dutch girl costume
daintily holding her braids out like wings,
her smile both demure and coy,
catching the eye of my Vaudeville grandfather
with his dark good looks and Chicago polish,
and running away with him
to life on the Pantages Circuit,
far from staid Waukegan,
a scandal even now to her clan
over a hundred years later, blessed woman
in marcelled curls.
Grandmother, dead of breast cancer
before my birth, I thank you for your flame.
I miss your monkey son

who hoped to reach 100
just three years shy,
never complaining of aches and pains.
"If you don't have health, you don't have anything,"
he used to say. Not wealth, not fame, but health.

I miss the old cherub
who would have delighted in the avenue
below my Granada hotel,
our name with the Moorish root,
transported by orange blossom and pear
and starry nights reflected in moon water
and the beatitude of time.

Each time I hear
the accordion player's song
annotating the past,
I long to enter his riddle,
lost to all knowing.

Oxnard—Granada—Oxnard *et. al*

> *"That which we call a rose by any other name would smell as sweet."*   Shakespeare

I
So what is this pedantry about a name?
Henry T. Oxnard, whose German name
means a bull's testicles,
sensibly thought *"Sugar"* a better appellation
than his own for the city
sprouting from his sugar beet factory,
whose bricks now line the walls of my yard
where cats walk in the after hours
and wind blows orange blossoms
from the citrus groves long ago replacing sugar beets;
but city fathers favored
Oxnard's own priapic name to guard its vineyards
on the plain.

Just so I am beguiled by Lorca's father
also grown rich from sugar beets
on Andalusia's plain,
as if this should signify,
for Henry T. Oxnard also spun American Crystal Sugar
from glacial soil in Minnesota, my home state.

II
Poplar forests dot the fields
around the Lorca sugar beet refinery
now used for breeding pigs
in Asquerosa, a place likewise wanting a name upgrade
from a problematic etymology—

"Disgusting"? Or *"Sweet Water"*?—

all of which resulted in *"Valderrubio, Valley of Light Tobacco,"*
to match the status of its famous citizen.

In Valderrubio's tiny auditorium
behind the Lorca family home
where a hologram of a Lorca-lookalike,
a ghost in a white suit, addresses tourists,
I dozed at the back among empty chairs.

Suddenly someone tapped my shoulder.
I awoke but no one was there,
only tourists seated at the front,
as if the oneiric poet himself had escaped his hologram
unable to endure
anyone napping in his presence;
or as if the chimera whose lovely name fits
inside the pocket of my own name
like a wafer in my mouth,
offered blessing before I sailed
home across the Atlantic
to Oxnard, cocooned in jet stream,
chastened by non sequitur and shadow.

Trip Advisor: Flamenco Show at *Le Chien Andalou*

Below the hills of Granada's gypsy quarter
on the river Darrow
in this tiny cave
named for Buñuel and Dali's film—**see above**—
black sounds gush from the old throat
of the *gitano* on stage,
his scorched voice wailing of love and disaster,
trolling his unguent guitar
and the dancer's feet
battering heart beats on the wooden floor.

In this popular venue
where I drink sangria companionably
with fellow tourists,
how is it the owner
has chosen to extol tragedy
with its title—**see above**—
when Buñuel hated gypsies,
not to mention Lorca's GYPSY BALLADS
and Dali rarely, if ever, visited Granada,
painting head after severed head of Lorca,
his first love?

What is the point of this misnomer
when the moon laughs at shadows,
a horn slipping through the pocket of night,
an ivory button half in, half out,
ready to undo time?

Nearby on the cathedral plaza
a cadre of men practice rising and walking
with their concrete roof that will carry the saint
during *Semana Santa*, while
teenage boys practice a smaller version,

pure theater,
like Dali and Buñuel's dream—**see above**—
which caused such anguish to Lorca
    with its sliced eye ball,
        and a man on a bicycle attired in woman's clothing
        sneered at by women,
that Lorca cried out, "*I am the Chien Andalou!*"
    And to add further horror,
    a bullet pierced that man,
    mocking the shot at Viznar where Lorca was to fall,
    like so many others of the Republic.

Ghosts haunt this cozy venue
where dancers no longer use castanets
and money brokers death.

Apotheosis at Viznar

"Why do you want to go to Viznar?"
asks the woman behind the tourist desk.
"There's nothing there, just a plaque."

Days later I catch the bus
toward the Sierra Nevadas,
passing Fernando del Ríos High School,
passing Cipriano de Rivas Street—
names from the Republic—
as the road curves upward
toward the village beloved of Moors
for its sweet winds and aqueducts
and where Moslem youth still walk after school.

And then the long walk in the hot morning
out of the white village along a quiet little road
with views of the Vega.
I am eager to hear birds
as the road curves by olive trees in bloom
and caves in the distance where I can just
see donkeys in their paddocks.
A bicyclist passes, then a couple.
I pass naked red cliffs
like those along the California coast.
Around a curve I suddenly arrive
at the steps to a semicircle
of unfinished blue and white plaques
for the Republican dead;
Lorca's name is missing.
I am glad for solitude
and the bird calls and water still trickling
in the aqueduct down to Granada.

In Lorca's time no sensible person took this route.
On his last night Lorca was taken from jail,
driven into these moonless hills
and deposited where I now walk
with only a bad photo,
looking for the old olive tree
and its nearby plaque.
The ground is lumpy still
where men and women were hastily buried
after a volley of shots,
their stone markers later cruelly
removed by civil authorities.
Finally, near a ditch, I see the old tree
and nearby, the plaque
looking like an overflowing trash
receptacle with dead flowers on top.
And there Lorca fell
wearing the loose tie of a poet.

Mexico City Sleight of Hand
(on seeing Mariachis for the first time)

In Mexico City
one summer afternoon,
in a taxi stuffed with Fulbright women
as if we were locked in steerage
and the golden angel over Reforma
was the Statue of Liberty,
we sped across the dusty city
roiling with hot humanity and car exhaust,
past the fire-eaters and jugglers, past
the preteen boys in the Zona Rosa promising
a shoeshine and oral sex,
until we neared our hotel
and the Street of *Novios* where bridal dolls
stared out of shop windows like zombies
reminding me that love and death
are synonymous;
just so, at the hour of swifts and vespers
we barely missed the drama
of a VW bug riven with bullets
the door hanging open,
its narrative lost.

Seventeen million people on this sinking island
but the ones who tumbled me
into dizzying, bracing waters
were the men in tight, silver studded suits
walking into traffic at the dinner hour
as if to offer, like streetwalkers,
not their siren guitars and a song,
but their surround sound masculinity.

Once in Tepotzotlán
for Paul Bowles

I
Once in Tepotzotlán
I slept in a blue house
that was wrapped in sadness,
sacrifice for the gods.
A gallery of birds swam in the wind
and the peacock
screamed in the trees
while the adjacent room
throbbed with a woman's weeping.

All afternoon
I sat on the long balcony
overlooking orchards,
entranced by green light
and the black walls
of the circular alley
while sobs and Gregorian chants
penetrated the paper walls
of the next room
and washed over my solitude,
as if I myself were an atom of sorrow
absorbed in prayer,
until, finally, the woman's husband
arrived from the capital,
summoned, as if from a bottle,
a dapper genie in a crisp suit,
not at all a stricken bird
like his wife,
to coo in her ear solemnities
of cricket song.

II
Alone at night in my own blue room,
snug amid cool sheets
I was troubled from slumber
by another song
wooing me awake
by some gigantic cicada
hidden in the walls,
some prehistoric insect
whose sudden atavistic nocturne
unleashed the moorings of my bed,
tumbling me headlong
into a ferment of dream and desire,
sea anemones fingering my body.

Outside my room
the banana plants
clattered in the wind at the balcony's edge
          and the hooves of riderless horses
walking down below in the dark lane
under the black trees,
under the black moon—
shadows passing behind thought—
          punctuated the hour.

Atala Addresses Her Aztec Gods

Open the legs of Mexico's nights
and you find oranges and stars,
our streets at dusk, garbage pickers,
fire eaters and drunken youths fighting
on streetcorners.

You enter and what happens next is another tale,
not for me to tell, only to imagine;
women are not to mind these heavy nights
beneath Xochiquetzal's* marigold skirts.

No one is there in her feathered cave, only the wind
you mistake for song, not peacocks
or hummingbirds but your wet kisses, Tlaloc,**
immense rain blossom,
whose petals fall on the flower vendor's trolly,
releasing the peppery scent of carnations.
But what do you know?
You thrust in and rain falls on Chapultepec.

And thunder, while I become
that tree, Queen of the Night
whose gold blossoms open and close.

* goddess of fertility
** god of rain

The Circular Valley

I
If I had slept, I would have
missed the horses
entering the lanes at midnight,
coming out of the hills
to wander through the silent town
on a secret nocturnal mission,
their hooves clattering quietly
over cobblestones, unhurried
in their movements, as gentle
as whispers. Their sweet
shadows lost in the dark trees,
they policed the town for the tricksy
God of Pulque spiriting
down from the mountain
to do mischief to our slumbers.

Before dawn an animal's cry
pierced my dreams, like a demon's
shriek outside my window, a squeal
of terror as life was torn
from its body, a savage matin
mocking the day.

II
Later as I walked the lanes, all
signs of slaughter had been cleared
away, the pig cleaned and quartered
for its ritual barbecue.

High up through the trees
loomed the mountain
I was going to climb,
its deceptively steep slope
hidden in vegetation,
until the last section
broke through, a pillar
of vertical rebar pounded
in stone. Along the way
I noticed little crosses
marking a death.
At the top through more
scrims of vegetation
hovered the little pyramid
dedicated to the ancient God of Pulque
whose spirit watched over the valley
and busied itself dreaming
up dangers for the unwary.

Amilcar Beach, Tunisia 1981

The boy watches for tourists
in the parking lot of Hotel Amilcar.
He waits for the old bandy-legged Frenchman
who struts up and down the beach
morning and evening.
I see the two of them later in the cafe
with its 180 degree views of this ancient coast.
The boy puts his hand on the Frenchman's
thigh and leaves it there.

Each morning I walk up and down
the beach too watching the white ferry
in the distance, crossing from Palermo
to Tunis and back again at dusk
to the Christian world.
Sometimes I hike up the hill
and follow the women with market baskets
to the best produce and bread.
Or I lie in the grass and watch the bumble bees
tackling the yellow four o'clocks,
their tiny quarterback legs padded with pollen.
Or I share a spoon over lunch
in sweet silence with the guardian
of the forest, *Sidi* Belquessem
who guards our van too
in the lot next to the wood and the hotel.
"*Sidi*" because he has been to Mecca.
We sit in his three-sided tin hut,
comfortable with each other.

One day *Sidi* herds
the muttering old Frenchman
out of the woods, where he
had gone with the boy. At night,
Sidi, with his empty sleeve in his pocket
walks his bicycle up the hill,
coasting down its steep incline in the morning,
his job as guardian a reward for war service.

After my weekly shower at the hostel
I too coast down the hill on my bike,
caught in the lip of the world.

Arab Vespers

I
Soon twilight will quiet the roosters
whose archipelagos sweeten
my *cafe au lait* on the hotel terrace
above the Bay of Tangier.
Traffic has not yet slowed as the hour
thrums with people winding
through the Casbah, laden with steaming
dinner pails of spicy *shakshouka*
and stopping at street corners
to scoop roasted chickpeas
into paper cones from wheelbarrow ovens.

II
Lingering on the terrace, watching
ferries from Gibraltar arrive in port,
I am happy to be where no one can find me.
I am not a polyglot
in this noisy crossroads; I have no voice,
no permanence, and at this hour, no shadow
as the coast lists upward to the plateau,
a ruffle in the continent, my life
a scroll unrolling and snapping shut at once,
its text invisible ink.

III
The bay now a necklace of lights
from late cars piercing the misty night,
in several more hours I will sleep,
only to be lulled from slumber
at three a.m. by the *muezzin's* call,
floating in its dark song,
a lullaby rising and falling in waves
over the bay, as plaintive as dream,
Prayer is better than sleep.
Prayer is better than sleep.

Matisse's "Window at Tangier 1912"

I

I arrive in Tangier by night.
The taxi noses through dark lanes
lit only by headlights;
pedestrians in white *djellabas*
float on the verge of the road
fading in and out like ghosts
leading to a secluded courtyard
covered in a cloud of red bougainvillea
and nutmeg, data of a new continent,
siren to my senses.   In the arcade
of the Grand Hotel Villa de France,
night is luminous and quiet, folding
me in its pocket.

II

Morning light cascades through the lace curtains
of Matisse's blue window into my hotel room;
it beckons down the lane
to the theater of the Petit Socco:
the stage fills with people
carrying market baskets through the city's gate,
calling me. "*Come down, oh, come down,*"
footsteps and voices a ululation
rising up from the English church
white and looming, with the fortune teller
in his little corner hut casting shadows.
The window says, "*You are here.*"

III

"*Go through,*" says this blue proscenium,
swinging open to admit me,
and I fly past the potted flowers on its sill
and up beyond the church
to the Casbah on the ramparts
and the sea and sky beyond,
Gibraltar barely visible through the eucalyptus—

scrim of blue shadows—
over the rooftops, to the cafes
and honey cakes and mint tea
in the Grand Socco where I watch humanity,
algorithm of the street.

IV
At night this scene draws in on itself,
falling action hushed in absolution,
the window a lapis curtain.
Below in the garden, the wind
and the white owl haunt the cypress tree,
ciphers of lost lessons from a lost script.

North Africa

Guide books warn
against entering the medina
without a *cicerone*,
but I relish a labyrinth
and go alone many times
through tortured streets
thronged with donkeys, men in *djellabas*,
and women in *burqas*,
haggling in the *souks* for scarves,
pinwheels of color,
eluding the touts,
and passing below latticed windows
where women, once sequestered,
looked down on life.

I love best the crenellated ramparts
and the huge ancient arches
tucked with pocket doors,
some mint green, some sky blue,
opening in to secrets.

One time a flood of spices lured me
to a *souk*
where bowls of little powdered tents
of curry, cumin and Chilies,
upstaged a table with a large jar
of dead Diptera labeled, *Spanish flies*.

Another time, at an imposing bronze door
I hazarded a knock,
hoping for the British Legation,
but which opened
to a blond god in jockey shorts
who had ingested herbs of his own.
He left me in a dazed caesura
while he drifted up the spiral staircase,

— for a robe—I assumed.
I lingered in the blue tiled foyer
wondering if I should leave.
But five minutes later he reappeared
still in fig leaf and vagaries,
directing me to another door
down the lane, less scenic.

There in the consular library
was a half-crazed missionary
gritting her teeth at being a *cicerone*
for two young novices
newly arrived in Tangier;
ever frugal, she invited me along
to share a taxi to Spanish Morocco.
We all met at her grim little flat
where clothes soaked
in the bathtub and desiccated plants
dangled from flower pots.
"*You must take me as you find me,*" said she.

In Tetuán she herded
us through the medina
with her eye on the clock,
allotting one hour only
in this city where Franco
began his assault on Spain decades ago,
and barking orders at us not to dawdle,
while all around us fountains
whispered of roses.

What is the Word for Surrender?

On the train from Fez to Tangier, I did not
understand why we stopped miles from any
city and we all had to exit. This wasn't a junction
or even a crossroads with ghosts or a byway
in which to lose one's self.
There was no sign saying, "*You are here.*"
Not knowing our spot on the map
I watched the train shrink into the horizon.

I hoped someone would join me on the platform to await
another train, but none tarried; instead all melted into thickets
bordering the track, spirits of the place only,
lacking even an echo.
In a distant eucalyptus grove a knot of ghostly adobes
huddled as if forgotten long ago.

I hoped I had heard right, had understood words
not said directly, that another train would arrive soon.
But what if I was wrong?

The wind whistled around me, the sun high overhead—
skeins of cloud in an azure sky of marble
paper. I turned this way and that, listening
to the silence of the continent,
vastness stretching forever.

Not even a fly buzzed. Would I die in this place?
I did not want to languish
here when shadows thickened, forced to approach
a cluster of houses that looked abandoned.

An hour passed. Finally I sat on my luggage,
watching the eucalyptus flutter in the afternoon,
the moments opening then closing, shriven
by wind, a leaf blown into ether.

Death in Tunisia

I
One spring we lived on the beach
in Sidi Bou Said,
below Amilcar Hotel;
morning and evening we walked on the shore
watching the ferry crossing the bay
to and from Palermo in blue infinities.

Beyond the hotel, a little port bobbed
with the tidy yachts of the rich
arriving from Europe
and buttoned to their moorings
like obedient ducks,
safe from wanderlust.

Above the port, the American ambassador's house
kept watch on the cliff
down which tumbled red, orange, and yellow
nasturtiums, flags warning
of a slippery slope in eucalyptus shadow.
An intruder did tumble there once and die.

I had a pet dog, Buddy, one of many strays
hanging out at the beach cafe,
a little brown female, eager
to get in our van during the rains.
On sunny days she sat on the beach
watching the waves, spellbound by distant tides,
murmurations of light and cloud.
I wanted to take her home,
but in those days my husband and I
were strays too.

II
One day I wandered between the port
and the camp ground
behind the hotel parking and came

upon a large square pit,
footprint remains of some abandoned building,
full of dank water. To my horror
and dismay a retriever floated there—
a hapless member of Buddy's tribe
guarding the beach cafe;
or some tourist's dog lost in the night
who, smelling the water, bounded forward,
plunging heedlessly into the void.
Every time I think of that dog
I have no words for its last moments,
stricken with panic and terror,
paddling back and forth looking
for a foothold, desperate for help
until finally, fatigue and weakness
overtook it.

Forty years later I still don't
know how to write about it,
wondering if it floats there still,
stark reminder of the many casualties of life,
and of the time we camped along the road
to the Sahara.

Before bedtime,
beguiled by the itinerant moonlight
drifting without a map in the night,
we walked across a sandy field,
the air filled with honeyed breezes
cooing to the universe.
Next morning, before resuming
our journey into the desert, we retraced
our footsteps in the hot blue light,
only to discover
a series of deep shafts in the ground,
bottomless unmarked wells along
the nocturnal route we had so blithely taken.

With Thanks

I owe my development as a poet to the many fine poets of Ventura County and its neighboring counties, who make California such a vibrant and welcoming place for writers. I am equally indebted to my Cigar Factor Lovelies for their wisdom and stimulation. It is my good fortune to be a part of these extended poetry communities.

Elaine Alarcón grew up in Anoka, Minnesota. She earned an M.A. and a Ph.D. in Creative Writing from the University of Denver, where she studied under John Williams and Robert D. Richardson. She has been nominated three times for a Pushcart Prize, has won the Woody Bartlett Poetry Prize twice, and also the Leon Priestnall Poetry Prize. Kelsay Books will publish her forthcoming poetry collection, RUM RIVER BALLADS. She now lives in California near the sea.

www.ingramcontent.com/pod-product-compliance
Lightning Source LLC
Chambersburg PA
CBHW022057080426
42734CB00009B/1383